1

Judged By 12

An Explanatory Account of the School to Prison Pipeline

By

Derrick Davis

I would like to thank the following...

First and foremost, I have to give thanks to my best friend, and my Co Chair at YouthMindsMatter, Khia Naylor. You have stuck by me throughout this entire process and many others while simultaneously balancing work, family, and reaching your own philanthropic goals at WBC (Women Breaking Chains). I know I've been a pain to work with at times and I appreciate your patience more than you'll ever know. Thanks for believing in my vision.

I also would like to thank my beloved Ma Dukes. I'm sorry for all the tears and heartache. I thank you, for always standing behind your oldest boy.

To my extremely independent sister, Shana. For being the best sister, one could ask for, and giving me a beautiful niece, and loyal nephew.

To my oldest nephew Quamir. I appreciate you answering my calls and keeping me alive on social media. I remember when I used to take you to my favorite breakfast spot and you would stand on my lap and eat your scrambled eggs with your hands. Now you've grown and are taller than me. I love you Quamir and I'm proud of you.

To My grandmother Grace Davis, and her late husband Terrell Davis. I thank you two so much for being a consistent positive in my life. Grandma you're the strongest women I've ever met. You lost your mother,

4

father, brother, and husband within a five-year span and still do not possess a pessimistic bone in your body. Thank you for your love and your wisdom.

To my younger brother Malcolm, keep your head up and stay focused. I understand your plight l'il bro, and it will get greater later.

To my baby sister Jamaica. I know we don't talk much but know I love you, and I'm always rooting for you.

To my beautiful Mother Dear, Lisa Davis. The epitome of a strong black woman. You always embraced me as I was your own, and shed light through some of my darkest days.

I would also like to dedicate this book to Booby Harris. My brother from another. You embraced me behind these walls and watched me grow from a boy into a young man, and I appreciate your loyalty, my friend.

To Helen Levin, and Mary Could. My lawyer, and mitigator who worked tirelessly with helping me secure a second chance at life on the other side of these walls. While tumultuous at times, it was a pleasure working with the two of you, and I appreciate the dedication, and sincerity you both brought to the table.

To my two-favorite activist, Liz Geyer and George Trudel, who're fighting tooth and nail to get lifers in PA a shot at parole. Keep up the hard work, and know you both are extremely appreciated amongst the men currently trapped behind these walls.

Lastly but not least, I have to thank Judge Barbara A. McDermott. Thank you so much for seeing me, and taking a shot on me, and giving me a second chance at life. You're a beast at what you do. Your stern, heavy handed conduct served its purpose, and helped me see that once indebted to society your work is never done.

Authors Note

I have tried to recreate events, locales and conversations from my memories of them.

In order to maintain their anonymity in some instances I have changed the names of individuals and places, I may have changed some identifying characteristics and details such as physical properties, occupations and places of residence.

Judged By 12

An Explanatory Account of the School to Prison Pipeline

Coming of Age

A 13-year-old Buck is lying on his mother's old couch inside the living room watching the television. His stomach is growling due to the fact he hasn't eaten anything all day except a bag of Hot Fries he'd picked up on his way home from school. He stood only 5'3 and weighed in at a mere hundred pounds, so he could go a day or two without a solid meal and be just fine.

Buck decides to try his hand and see if "Ma Dukes" has a few extra coins in order for him to treat himself to a chicken wing platter from the Chinese store. He yells up the dark stairs.

"Maaaa!!!"

He immediately regretted yelling, and wished he'd chose to just walk up there and ask her. Before he could finish his thoughts, his worries were confirmed by the annoyance in Ma Dukes voice when she responded.

"What boy? Why the fuck is you yelling in my house?"

"I'm hungry. I need some money so I can get something to eat from the Chinese store."

The silence that followed gave Buck a sense of hope, almost to the point he could smell the ketchup and hot sauce on those wings. Only to be crushed by Ma Dukes reply.

"Boy you better find something to eat in this house, and I don't want to hear that the fridge is empty. It's something down there".

A pissed off Buck walks out of the house. He has a dollar in his pocket, and decides to just settle for an egg roll from the Chinese store. He sees S. an older guy from his block who he'd been watching for as long as he could remember.

S. was considered and Old Head. He stayed in some Gucci loafers, slacks and button up shirts, and he keep a pair a gold Cartier frames. S. was known for two things... Gambling, and beefing over some young chicks.

Sitting in the driver's seat was his number one young bull, Rahman. Rahman was the complete opposite of S. Rahman was all about stacking his coins, and planning for what's next, opposed to S. who lived in the now.

They were both sitting in Rahman's new Black Cadillac CTS that S. had all but forced him to buy, listening to Rahman's favorite rapper Jay Z.

Buck wishes he was in there with them as he walks by the car, and high steps into the Chinese store, trying to get out of the cold a few seconds sooner. He then makes up his mind to holla at them once he leaves the store. S. always says something to him, so this time he would put his bid in and sees if they would put him on.

As he passes the Caddy, he hears the window slide down and like clockwork S. checks in with him.

"What it is young fella? I see you got ya'self an egg roll."

A nervous Buck wanting to sound cool responds.

"Yeah, I was hungry as shit."

S. and Rahman both laugh, and S. tells Rahman to give Buck a few dollars. Buck accepts the 20$ from Rahman and walks away, pissed at himself for not working up the heart to ask them to put him on.

As S. watches Buck in the rearview mirror walk back towards his house, he glares over at Rahman.

"It's something about that young bull that I dig. It's only a matter of time before he jumps off the porch, and I'm thinking about putting him on with us. What you think?"

Rahman playing with the zipper on his black Mark Buchanan leather jacket, matching his car, bracing for the argument he knows to come.

"Man, I like the young bull, but he's young as shit. Plus, he lives on the block, so how you think his folks gonna respond to that?"

S. gives a disappointed smirk before letting Rahman have it.

"The Sanctimonious Rahman! My main man with the selective memory. When I was your age, guess whose age you were? That's rhetorical niggah. You were his age. I put you on then and look at you now, sitting in this soft butter. It's best he gets down with us now before these lames scoop him up. At least he'll be getting some real paper over. Give him a squirrel (7 grams) and show him what to do wit it. His folks won't say shit, how can they? The young niggah is eating an egg roll for dinner."

Rahman shaking his head.

"Say less."

Product of Environment

TWO YEARS PASS BY, AND BUCK IS NOW LIKE FAMILY TO RAHMAN AND S...

Buck enters the crack house he frequents daily in order to make his routine drops. The smell of Newports and crack in the air is burning his nose.

He tightens up a few of his regulars, and sees the neighborhood trick Lisa Lips sitting at the top of the raggedly old steps.

She's wearing her favorite one-piece red body suit, and no shoes. Buck immediately bricks up, but tries to play it cool, all the while knowing he's gonna break and give her a few dimes for a quickie as he always does.

Lisa had a hold on Buck being as tho she was his first. She had him light years ahead of his age when it came to the bedroom. His dark skin, and his long braids would always get him in the door with the fast-assed neighborhood girls, and his lessons from Lisa Lips would have them hooked.

Lisa Lips spotting her opportunity for her free play of the day jumped at it.

"Hey Buck Buck! I didn't know that you were stopping by. I know you wasn't gonna come here and not even speak to me."

Buck never one to miss a jab.

"I saw your daughter in school yesterday; did she tell you we're getting married?"

A pissed off Lisa Lips stood up, but before she could think of her retort, Rahman entered the crack house.

"What is taking you so long? I know ya nasty ass be in here tricking, Buck. You out of pocket, ya dick gonna fall off you keep messing with these weenies."

Buck embarrassed Rahman knew his secret, just laughed it off, but recognized some worry on Rahman's face.

"What's wrong bro?"

Rahman motions Buck to follow him with a nod, and they leave the crack spot.

"Listen S. got booked last night. I spoke to him this morning and we're gonna have to get some coins up and pay his lawyer."

A baffled Buck asked. "Why would we need to pay his lawyer? S. was getting more cheese than the both of us, so I'm prey sure he's covered. Plus, why not just bail him out?"

Rahman playing with his zipper as he usually does when he's thinking things through.

"Buck, man S. is locked up for a body, and there's no bail for a body. Plus S. didn't put no money up. All his money went to the gambling houses, the casinos, and of course the hoes."

They both immediately break out into laughter and simultaneously blurt S's favorite line... "You ain't a gangsta until you fall in love wit a hoe!"

After regaining his composure Rahman gets back to the business at hand.

"Seriously tho, Buck. Things are gonna change from here on out. S. gotta be able to count on us. We're his team, we're family, and if we don't stand on that shit, then we're no better than the rest of these nothing ass niggahs that we have to operate around out here. They forget their so-called homies the minute they're out of sight.

We're built different lil bro, we stand behind ours 100%, and we gonna make sure he's good. With that said he put the old head Boo down at the dice game, and Boo's brother Boobie is a problem. I don't have the rest of them dudes up there going too hard, but Boobie we have to worry about. I know this is new to you, so I'm gonna handle it, but make sure you stay on point."

Buck realizing that he's entering unknown territory decides to speak his piece.

"I'm gonna keep it a buck wit you. That shit got me super nervous, but wit S. gone, you all I got out here, and if you push then I'm gonna push wit you. I can't imagine being out here by myself, and y'all showed me nothing but love from day one, so count me in." Rahman responds. "Say less".

Rahman then turns up Jay Z's "Crew Love", lights a backwood and passes it to Buck as they listen to Jay tear over the hook.

"You know it's crew love - Roc-A-Fella till we die - As long as you and I keep it movin' like a drive by - We can stack doe sky high - Niggahs can't touch what they can't feel - Real recognize real."

A YEAR PASSES AND RAHMAN & BUCK ARE SITTING IN RAHMAN'S CADDY EATING WENDY'S...

Buck with a mouth full of fries.

"We gotta find a new late-night spot. I'm getting burnt out eating this shit every night."

Rahman laughs... "I agree li'l bro, I think there's a---". Boom! Boooom Booooom Boooom!!!!! Shots fly rapidly as Buck rolls out of the passenger side door fumbling at his waist, trying to free his P89 Ruger. He sees the black tinted up Crown Victoria spending away as he's able to lift his gun and fire his entire clip.

He jumps in the Caddy and notice Rahman is hit.

"Rahman! Rahman! Get the fuck up bro."

A knot swells in his chest at the thought of his best friend, his brother being dead. He pulls Rahman into the back seat and speeds off to the nearest hospital. While waiting for the doctors to let him know something, Rahman's mom enters the hospital along with his li'l brother, and his girl. Buck looks at her, and she returns his worried look. Ms. Agnus always looked at Buck as another son, and he looked another as another mother.

"Did they say anything yet?"

Buck shakes his head while staring at his bloody hands.

"Mom, I know you don't want to hear this but I promise you if he doesn't come up out of this, I'm gonna play my part for him."

A disappointed Ms. Agnus responds in her stoic tone.

"Buck you know I love you, and all I ask is for you to just stop. Right now, it's me; tomorrow it's your mom, the day after its someone else's mother.

Y'all have to stop. It's too much for any mother to bear, and if you love me, and you love your mom the way we love you, then you would stop."

The doctors come out and pronounce Rahman dead. They all break down and cry.

In the midst of the tears, Buck failed to notice the two detectives off to the side speaking with the nurse. Had he looked up he'd noticed that sell out ass Detective Jenkins. Jenkins had been harassing him ever since S. got booked, and was known to play dirty. He tried his best to look like the in crowd, with his corny ass beard dyed black and wavy hair. He approaches Buck.

"We need to talk."

Rahman's girlfriend Mercedes, who looks at him as a brother immediately steps in.

"My husband was just killed and y'all lost y'all mind if y'all think y'all gonna harass my li'l brother right now. Damn can we grieve?"

Annoyed, Detective Jenkins ignores her, grabs Buck by the arm and escorts him to the homicide division. As soon as Buck enters the double doors, he recognizes a face on a wanted poster, and thinks to himself.

Damn that's Mill Mill, they on his ass. I hope they don't catch 'em.

Detective Jenkins handcuffs Buck to the table and searches him. Buck remembered to toss the guns but forgot he had a bundle of crack in his pocket. Jenkins removes the bundle and slaps in on the table without acknowledging it, and looks Buck in his eyes before asking him.

"So, what happened, Buck?"

Feeling offended by the detective referring to him by his government handle, he snidely corrects him.

"Buck? My name is Derrick, and I don't know what happened. As you know, I live on the block. I heard shots, and I looked out the window and saw it was Rahman, so I ran up there to make sure he was straight. He wasn't, so I took him to the hospital, and called his folks up."

Jenkins sat back preparing to gauge Buck's response when he drops his next bomb shell on him.

"So, answer this. Why is there a black Crown Victoria found shot up with a dead body in it a block away from where your friend... Rahman is it?"

"Rahman." Buck fires back.

"Yeah Rahman. Where Rahman was shot, and why was there two different sets of shell casings out there? Hold on this is the kicker. The dead body that was Jason Smith, also known as Boobie.

Who is that you may ask? Well that's the brother of James Smith also known as Boo; may he rest in peace. Now it's coming together right? Your old head Solomon, better known as S., is serving a 20-year sentence for killing Boo. You see where this is going?"

Struggling to keep his game face on after learning that he just killed Boobie shoots back.

"Yeah it sounds like you did your homework, but I don't know what you want from me. I just lost my best friend and now I'm cuffed to this nut ass table, listening to you do the Sherlock Holmes thing. I can't help you. Can I go?"

A pissed off Jenkins foreseeing the harassment to come from his colleagues for not being able to crack a 17-year-old.

"We can't prove that you had anything to do with it right now, but we will be talking again. In the meantime, I'm gonna make sure the Judge sends your young ass to juvie for the bundle of crack you had on you."

Buck just shakes his head, still dazed from the fact that he lost this best friend, and caught his first body all in the same night.

Entering the System

BUCK IS IN A JUVENILE DETENTION CENTER READING
A LETTER FROM HIS MOTHER.

*Man, Ma Dukes loves her boy. I get a kite from her
weekly. I gotta get back out there and help her with my
sisters and brother tho.*

*When I walked out from the back and into the
courtroom, and heard my little sister scream by name,
"Derrick!!!!" in the sweetest little voice, that shit broke
me. I miss them so much.*

*Damn! I still can't believe Rahman is gone. We were
out there lunching heavy, and we knew better. Them
clowns from them block stood by and did nothing. I
know they think it's over for our team but they got
another thing coming.*

*Shit gonna change when I get out. They seen how I
moved, plus putting the work in was way easier than I
thought it was, and now I know for sure what I'm cut
like, so I know I can pick up where we left off and take
this shit to another level.*

*I just hope that the plug trusts me enough to put me
on, and front me the same thing he was fronting
Rahman after S. got booked. All in all, shit definitely
gonna change tho.*

As Buck is laying on his bunk, he hears a strange, yet peaceful chant.

"Allaaaahu Akbar, Allaaaaaahu Akbar," He puts his letter down and continues to listen until the end. "Laaaaa ilahaaa illalaw."

He then walks to the door in order to make eye contact with the dude who was making the chant.

"Wassup wit you? I heard you over there signing or something. What was that?"

The guy who would later identify as Nell was clearly offended by the singing comment. The black mark on his forehead instantly wrinkling from his frown.

"I wasn't signing, I was calling the adhan. That's the call to let all the Muslims know that it's time to pray. My name is Nell, and if you want, I can send you some books over that my pop sent me. Where you from?"

Not wanting to seem over friendly, but clearly interested in the religion accepts the offer.

"My name is Buck, I'm from Southwest."

A surprised Nell responds. "O yah? I'm from West but both of my walkies are from your end. I'm not sure if you know them tho."

Buck knowing, he recognized the light skinned one with the snagged teeth and devilish grin, chooses to lie.

"Naw. I see them with you but I don't know them. Why is the light skinned one always smiling tho?"

Nell grins, and waives them over, informing Buck that the light skinned one is Dez, and he smiles because he doesn't have all of his marbles.

"I'm gonna introduce y'all. Dez and Seek this is Buck. He's from y'all end of town."

On cue, Dez acknowledges seeing Buck around.

"Yah, I used to see you when I go would to the pizza store. Y'all used to be parked up in that bombed out Caddy, and the trap was jumping down there. What happened?" Not liking where the conversation was going, Buck responds. "Long story."

TEN MONTHS PASS AND NELL, SEEK, DEZ, & BUCK ARE WATCHING VIDEOS IN THE AUDITORIUM...

Buck is picking at Seek for claiming he gets more chicks than him. Seek was a mirror image of Buck, especially since Buck cut his braids off. They were both relatively short standing at around 5'6, and both slightly stocky build, with brown eyes. The only characteristic with them that differed was Buck's incoming beard, which he never missed the opportunity to throw in Seek's face.

"Seek. Real shit. How you figure you get more hoes than me? You don't even eat pussy niggah. I can tell by the lack of hair on your face. I guarantee you, if your bitch hears about this legendary tongue, I'll take her too."

Seek, clearly pissed, focuses in on Dez.

"Dez is fuckin with the Pittsburgh niggahs again. He hates them dudes because they are in to that gang bangin shit. He feels like they have to gang up because they can't stand alone."

Feeling the atmosphere beginning to become tense, Buck positions himself for what's next. As Buck and Seek inch closer to Nell and Dez, Dez gets up and kisses Amastad on the back of his head.

Amastad was at least 6' 180, and as black as night. Anybody could tell that he'd been through his share of battles just by taking notice of the scars on his face and the missing front tooth.

Seek and Buck exchange a look that would become all too familiar. As Amastad cornered the isle to approach Dez. A little dude from Philly runs up behind him and punts Amastad straight up his ass. As the entire auditorium erupted in laughter, Amastad turns around.

"PUSSY!!!"

Crack!!!

He knocked the little dude clean out, and silenced the entire auditorium. As he turned back around Dez caught him with a flush over hand right, and stumbled him just enough for his team to get by his side. A

Pittsburgh vs. Philly riot brakes out, and they are all placed on lock down.

While on lockdown Buck takes the opportunity to pick Seeks brain, since they're now roommates.

"Damn bro, ya man Dez is all the way shot out. He got the whole camp locked down. I'm not even mad tho, I'm just glad that this shit is coming to an end. You leave in two weeks, right? What you got lined up?"

Seek, laying on his bunk with his hands behind his head, staring at the ceiling.

"Man, as you know my um passed away while I was here, so I'm gonna move in with my G mom. She's old now, but she doesn't get in the way of me doing me. You know what's crazy? She lives a block over from you. Hopefully once you touch down, we can link up."

Happy that Seek beat him to the punch.

"Yeah that sounds about right to me homie. My old head is fresh on a 20-year bid, and my right hand got smoked the same night that I got booked, so I'm gonna need somebody that I can count on once I touch down.

Niggahs been eating off the work we put in, and that shit is gonna change ASAP. I'm claiming the spot I earned out there, and they gonna follow suit."

Seek sits up and assures Buck that he's on deck.

"Man, I got you. Plus, I get out before you, so I'll make sure you're situated before you even get out. What about Nell and Dez tho?"

Buck hangs a picture of his girl, Butta on the wall beside his bunk, before regaining his focus on the conversation at hand.

"They cool. Dez is just a live wire, and I've seen how that turns out, so even tho I twist with him, I don't want to sit at the table with him. Nell on the other hand is my guy, and we already out some plans together, but being as tho Dez is his right hand, we had to set limits to how far we mob together. Insha Allah we'll all be straight tho."

Boys Become Men

SIX MONTHS PASS AND 18-YEAR-OLD BUCK IS NOW
HOME AND TALKING TO SEEK....

Buck sits on Seek's grandmother's couch, and
immediately complains.

"Bro why do ya grand mom got this hot ass
plastic on her couch, and how many pictures of Jesus
does she need in here?"

Seek knowing that Buck would bitch out calls his
grandma.

"Aye G! Buck has a few questions for you.

Stunned that Seek really just put him on the spot, Buck
digs deep for a response as Seek's grandma enters the
doorway.

"Hey Ms. Williams. Ya boy used to talk about
your card games, I just wanted to know if it was okay
for me to stop by, and join the game?"

Ms. Williams knowing something more was going on,
but not having the patience, nor inclination to deal
with their bullshit.

"Sure boy. What's your name again? Buck? Like a
damn deer? Just make sure you bring enough money to
pay the house."

Buck smirks and looks at Seek, with his big dumb ass grin on his face.

"Seriously tho bro. I appreciate you keeping your word. The wheel and the hammer you gave me is sufficient. I had some coins put up before I got booked, plus I spoke with the plug, and he says he's gonna throw some work my way, so we're gonna be good.

I didn't even say nothing to them dudes on the block yet, because I want to get with Chicken Man about that first. So, let me put some time in with Butta then I'm gonna get wit you. She rode that bid out wit me, so I got to make sure I put some time in with her before things get too deep out here. Just sit tight tho, I got you."

Eagerness was all over Seek's face.

"Sounds good to me. Did you say Chicken Man tho? Don't old head smoke crack? Fuck good, is he?"

Offended that Seek is questioning him regarding his own neighborhood, patiently explains.

"Yeah S. put me on him a while back. He was a hitta for S., and from what S. told me his hand was heavy way back when.

All in all, I know that he has the pearls I need to get in position and pull this off. So, I'm gonna check in with him and see where his head is at."

With his worries now at ease, Seek agrees. They shake hands and part ways.

Buck pulls into the parking lot of the neighborhood deli. Taking note that nothing has changed since he's been away. The same old drunks, and crack heads out here pissing behind the dumpsters, and taking hits inside the deli's dingy old bathroom. He knew that Chicken Man wouldn't be far from the scene.

Chicken Man was the crack head who all the other crack heads who'd been around feared. A real dirty Harry type nigga. His scruffy beard and way too thick mustache reeked with malt liquor, and smoke. His oversized jeans were covered in grit, and his raggedly button up shirt marked with stains and wet spots from the perspiration his tall boy produced.

Buck couldn't miss him as he wobbled out of the deli, with his signature tall boy clenched to his chest as if somebody would run by and snatch it.

"Got damn Buck Buck, is that you? When did you come home?"

A smiling Buck responds.

"Aw man. I just got out a couple weeks ago. Jump in tho I got some rap for you."

Buck immediately regretting his words but knowing it was too late to stop him from jumping in. Chicken Man jumps in with the same worries as Buck.

"Hadn't had a chance to freshen up young blood pardon me."

Feeling bad for the old timer, he assures Chicken Man that everything is cool.

"No worries. I'm gonna get you a fresh lay, and some new routes for your feet. I'm gonna rent you a room also. S. told me that I could count on your advice whenever he isn't around, and now I need you."

Happy to hear that his reputation had proceeded him. Chicken Man sits back, and rests his head on the headrest.

"Yeah S. has been my guy since way back when. He knows me, but to tell you the truth young buck. I would have backed your play without his stamp.

I know that you put the work in on the night Rahman got killed, and I also know that you kept your mouth shut, so that alone is enough for me. Plus, I watched you grow up out here. So, what's on ya mind?"

At his wits end with the stench, Buck chooses to wrap the conversation up.

"Let's get you cleaned up first big homie, and then we'll talk."

Chicken Man nods, and pulls out his pipe.

"You mind if I hit this really quick?"

31

Buck gives him the go ahead, knowing that he didn't want him smoking that shit in his car.

A FEW DAYS LATER...

Buck and Seek enter the dimly lit bar, with some old ass Barry White blaring over the speakers.

"Only Chicken Man".

Buck says while shaking his head, and feeling out of place, all the while looking around for Chicken Man.

"Is that him in the corner with the niggah Manzy? Make sure you're on point. I'm not sure why he's wit ole boy, so keep an eye on him."

Seek acknowledges his marching orders, as Chicken Man waves them over.

"Let me start by addressing the elephant in the room. Manzy is here because I know him and I trust him. I watched him grow up, just as I did you.

I know in your eyes he's a part of the problem, but I'm telling you he's not, and I need you to trust me on that."

A cautious Buck agrees and proceeds with the meeting.

"Crazy thing is this. I saw you at the Masjid for the Friday prayer when I first got out the juvie joint. I wanted to say something because I knew what I had planned but I didn't feel comfortable transgressing against my brother.

So, I was hesitant to look your way knowing we were just standing in the ranks together. So, the better part of me is glad that you're here today."

Manzy wasn't intimidating in any way. His short, round, pudgy like demeanor screamed nothing short of harmless, even tho he would do his best to make those around him believe he could put it in with the best of them. He didn't fool Buck, and he must have known it because it didn't even attempt to.

"I'm glad to hear that Akhi. I know you feel some type of way that we didn't move when Rahman got smoked, but you have to look at it from both sides. Y'all had been out there eating for years… years before you even linked up with them, and never did y'all extend us a hand.

We were cracked out there, fiends walking by us while we're standing in the cold to cop off of y'all sitting behind some tint in front of some heat. So, there was some bad blood.

Plus, I'm gonna keep it a real wit you, I'm not even into that shit. I'm about these coins and that's it."

Chicken Man sensing Buck's rage at the comments about his lost brothers cuts in.

"And we respect that. We have no choice but to. It shows that you're solid, and it shows that you know your role.

Most of these pups are out here frauding, and they're acting like they are something that they really ain't.

So, when you find a dude who knows his role, and is comfortable in that then you have to respect that."

Knowing that the rap was authentic, even if it didn't apply to this niggah in front of him, Buck chooses to stay on track.

"I'm picking up what you putting down ole timer. So, what's next?"

A twitchy Chicken Man goes into his game plan, bar for bar.

"So, Manzy tells me that the block is beefing wit some cats from the bottom. Vicious little dudes, but just so happens their old head is my young bull, and he will squash that beef the minute I ask him to do so.

So, they usually ride around in a tinted up Grand Marquis. I found one just like it. I want you to buy that car and get the windows tinted."

Buck realizing where this is going chimes in.

"I see where you going wit this. So, when we put the work in, they think it was them and not us."

Chicken Man agrees.

"Exactly so if they rat then it won't be on us. The tall niggah is the problem so we need to make sure he catches everything."

Chicken Man was referring to Rain Man. A tall arrogant lame, with a lazy eye. Dude seemed stuck in the 90's still rocking his hat to the back, but none the less he wasn't a bitch, and needed to all the way out of the way.

Chicken Man continuing his spiel.

"We then let the rest of them know that we squashed that beef for them. With Rain Man out the way, they'll be more than happy to hear that the heat is off they ass.

We let them know that they will be getting the work from Manzy, and Manzy will grab from you and only you. Work smarter not harder young buck."

Buck realizing how much things are about to change.

"Sounds like a game plan to me. So, what's next?"

Buck and Seek with Chicken Man at the wheel pull up to the light in the look alike Grand Marquis. They slide by slowly so everyone out on the corner recognizes the car. All eyes are glued to the car as Chicken Man spins the corner.

"Y'all jump out and wait two minutes before y'all start creeping around the corner. I'm gonna spin back around the block and sit at the light where they can see me.

That way while they're focusing on the car waiting to see what's next y'all can get up close from behind. Don't miss the target tho."

Buck excited at Chicken Man's game plan jumps out with Seek. After two minutes pass, they began to creep up behind the opposition.

Rain Man clutches his pistol as he keeps his eyes locked on the Grand Marquis.

"I wish these niggahs would try to he one off down here just like that."

For some odd reason Rain Man begins to turn around, and Seek lifts his 45. Chicken Man revs the engine and secures Rain Man's attention once again. Buck and Seek get close enough... Pop!

Poppppppoppooppooppopopopooooop!

Everybody scatters except the target. Mission accomplished.

Last "Tastes" of Freedom

YEARS PASS BY…

Buck finds himself more comfortable in his role with each day that passes by. He continues to build his reputation throughout Philly, and stacks his money like his best friend always advised him to. He never forgets his brother he'd lost to these mean streets, and he vows to never be the one on the wrong side of the gun.

He keeps in mind how the tables have turned, and he does everything in his power to prevent them from turning on him. He also does his best to keep a low profile while stacking his coins. He pulls up to the neighborhood car lot.

Sitting out front is the car dealer, Herb. At 6' 350 pounds easily. Herb reminds Buck of Heavy D, and he gets a laugh at his expense every time they cross paths.

"What's good Herb?"

Buck says. Herb lights up knowing he's finally about to get in Buck's pockets.

"What it is Bucky Raw?"

A kind of annoyed now Buck retorts.

"Why you call me that? Y'all niggahs got a hundred different versions of my name. I'm trying to grab a new wheel for the low. So, what you got for me?"

Herb all but drooling over the sell he's about to make.

"It's about time you're ready to step your game up. I got this BMW that fits you like a condom."

Buck smirks knowing he's not buying no damn BMW.

"That sounded gay, big homie, but how much for that Lincoln?"

A disappointed Herb responds. "For you? Give me ten".

Buck not up for the haggling.

"For me? Niggah that's the price on the window. I got eighty-five for you."

"Give me nine and it's yours." says Herb.

Ready to pull off, Buck says "I only got eight".

Herb sensing he's about to lose his only sale of the day accepts the eighty-five hundred dollars, after accusing Buck of short changing him. Before pulling off Buck decides not to miss his opportunity to jab Herb. He musters up his best Heavy D imitation, and drops it on Herb.

"I got nothing but love for you, baby". He laughs and pulls off.

It's late night. Buck and Seek met up with Nell and Dez, their other homies from the juvie joint.

Buck loves catching up with Nell, and even Dez when he's not being a dickhead. They pull up at KFC, and jump out of Buck's new Lincoln.

"Man, I went to KFC out by the mall last week, and their chicken was ten times better than this spot."

Buck says knowing he's about to start a debate. Like clockwork Nell takes the bait.

"All KFCs use the same ingredients; so how is that?"

Buck not going to back down.

"I thought the same thing, but I got this spot being on some ghetto shit, and serving us leftovers or something. I wouldn't be surprised, they only got one cashier and one cook.

Looks like they're trying to save some cheese if you ask me. Whatever the case may be, that shit was better. I know I wasn't tripping."

Seek not one for debates.

"Man, chicken is chicken."

All eyes turn to Dez scratching his head. They all thought they'd dodged a bullet. The bullet being his two cents.

"Man, is this niggah suggesting that white people cook better 'fried chicken' than black people?"

They all burst out laughing and order their food. Dez approaches the register and orders his five wings and a biscuit, but they all recognize that signature smirk on his face, and brace for the nonsense to follow.

"Give me some ketchup packs too."

Dez say as rudely as he could. The cashier walks over to the condiments and grabs a hand full of ketchup for him. He then demands.

"Get me some hot sauce too!"

The cashier now clearly annoyed walks over and get him a handful of hot sauce packs.

"I need some butter too, for my biscuit."

Buck annoyed, and feeling sorry for the girl who he sees daily, tries to spare her.

"Man, just tell her everything you need so we can get the fuck out of here."

Not one to fold, Dez doesn't budge.

"Hold up captain save a hoe. You ever had jelly and butter on ya biscuits? Shit is everything bro. Oh yeah. I need some honey too, sis."

The cashier frowns and slams the condiments on the counter. Dez jumps at the moment.

"Bitch why the fuck is you making that face? What you just looked at ya pay check? Be mad at ya boss not me."

They all laugh even tho every last one of them felt sorry for the girl. Dez gives her six dollars for his meal that costs 5.85 and tells her to keep the change.

Buck slides her a ten when Dez isn't looking and winks at her. She smiles as they leave the store.

They all are sitting on the block eating their chicken on the hood of Buck's car, when Aunty walks up.

Aunty was really like an aunt to Buck. He dealt with her on a daily basis and she reminded him so much of his mom's youngest sister. She was loud, and ashy, but she was the sweetest, most caring lady you'd ever meet.

Buck also went to school with her oldest daughter, Ebony who had teased him with the pussy one night, and had his balls in the most pain the next morning after failing all night to get the va jay.

"Sup, Aunty?" Buck said greeting her.

"Nothing sweetness. I do need you to talk to Flea, and the rest of them little bastards. I told them to stop calling me when I walking through here with my kids, and they keep doing it."

Buck responds feeling some type of way but trying to hide it.

"I got you. You want a piece of chicken?"

Buck hands Aunty a piece of chicken.

Poppoopppoooopoooooopoppppp!

"What the fuck?" Nell says as everybody stays put being as though the shots were at least a block away. Nell continues.

"Man, that's why I don't like chilling down here, it's always hot down here. These dudes do more shooting than they do getting money."

Seek in agreement chimes in.

"Yeah. I think that was the young bulls up the street. They was making one of them rap videos when we rode by, and I saw some unfamiliar faces. You want to slide up there and see what's what?"

Buck cutting in before Dez can answer.

"Nah, fuck 'em. It ain't us. Where the hell did Aunty go?"

Seek being the only one with the answer, does so.

"She hauled ass up the ally."

Everybody laughs except Dez.

Dez unleashes.

"Fuck the young bulls? You out here feeding crack heads, yet the li'l niggahs out here in the trap, in the trenches like we were, it's fuck them. Yeah, I'm lost on that one. Plus, I saw you slide that ignorant ass bitch some cheese at KFC. What time you on out here bro?"

Buck fed all the way up with Dez's bullshit responds.

"Aye Dez. Fuck is you talking to like that? I'm on my time niggah. I don't owe you shit, not even an explanation. You a dumb ass niggah Dez. What stand up niggah runs around terrorizing females, except ya goofy ass?

That crack head could be ya mother niggah. I got plenty of folks who smoke that shit, and niggahs better give them the same treatment I'm out here giving their folks.

Matter fact my old head, Chicken Man is a crack head, and I would love to see you call him one to his face."

Nell trying to cut the tension.

"Preeeeach!"

But Buck not letting Dez off that easy.

"Seriously, you a fuckin idiot bro."

Before things could get any more out of hand, Gena and her best friend Taryn pulls up in Gena's white Audi banging Beyoncé. She rolls down the window.

"Y'all good? We heard they was just shooting down here. That wasn't you was it?"

Buck still hot at Dez, but nonetheless happy to see Gena assures her it wasn't them and everybody is good.

Buck had the biggest crush on Gena, and he knew she was on his top also. Her sister deserved the cock block of the year award because she would lie and tell everybody she was messing with Buck, knowing them hood chicks wouldn't try her hand. But Buck lusted heavy for her sister, Gena.

Gena was about his height at 5'6, and had the fattest ass, and the cutest face to match. She kept some tights on with no panties, knowing every niggah wanted to see that wagon bare. For some reason she would make Buck sweat for it, but would never break for him.

Gena knowing, she had Buck where she wanted him starts playing her mind games.

"Somebody has been asking about you Buck."

Knowing who she was talking about and immediately getting frustrated he responds.

"Who CeCe? Yeah, I heard. I'm sure the entire hood knows that by now. I'm trying to see what's up with you tho. I been on ya top for how long, and you know I feel some type of way that you gave the young bull some pussy. Let me find out you like the young bulls."

Gena not missing her chance to rub it in.

"I like what I like."

44

Buck keeps his cool, and shoots back.

"Well I guess you don't like real niggahs huh?"

Gena feeling that Buck is just about done with her games tries to be transparent.

"It ain't that Buck. I'm just not trying to step on my sister's toes. We live by the girl code."

Dez jumps in, while keeping in mind that Buck is tight with this chick and not to take it too far.

"We live by the G code too."

They all share a laugh then Gena asks them.

"Are y'all going to the 5200 club tonight? Willie is having a fund-raising party to pay for Little Willies lawyer. You know he's trying to give his life sentence back. Y'all coming?"

Buck bricking up at the thought of getting some chill time with Gena shares.

"Yeah me and Seek are coming. Dez and Nell made plans for Onyx."

Dez then informs them that they can join them at the city's number one strip club. Gena declines and Taryn leans over her ensuring her next words would be heard loud and clear. Her pretty, yet hardened light skinned face with a red star tattooed under her left eye glowing through the darkness, she screams.

"We strictly dickly you bitch ass niggah."

They all burst out laughing, even Dez, as Gena pulls off.

Buck and Seek enter the 5200 club. As usual they throwing jabs at each other. Buck was getting on Seek for wearing his best watch, a Rolex Oyster, with a bust down bezel to the local club, and Seek was getting on Buck for never dressing up.

In Buck's eyes, his heavy-duty thermal shirt from the army and navy store, and fresh pair of Seven jeans were sufficient. His six-inch Timberland Boots were fresh, and he was at peace with his over the counter Calvin Klein watch, his wife brought for him. Seek on the other hand felt the need to pull out his Prada blazer, oversized clear Gucci frames, and that dumb ass attention grabbing watch.

They pull up at a table, and order drinks. After some meaningful conversation, Buck's worries are no longer legit, when he she's Gena strutting straight toward him and Seek. He can tell by the force in her walk that she's had a few and her well-deserved confidence is on a bean.

Without hesitation she sits on Buck's lap ohh so gentle. Buck rubbing her thighs and not thinking clearly says the wrong thing.

"What CeCe gonna say about this?"

Gena not one to turn away from what she wants, shots back.

"We can cross that bridge when we get there. Taryn not drinking so she can take my car tonight, and you can take me home."

Buck not about to blow it, takes her up on her offer immediately. He downs the remainder of his Grand Marnier, and Henny mix, and lifts his glass to Seek to acknowledge his departure.

"Seek my man, you enjoy your night."

Buck and Gena step into her mother's house. Buck phone goes off and Gena panics, exposing the fact that they might be crossing that bridge she'd referred to at the club.

"You gonna wake my sister up with that loud ass phone. She already mad that it was her night to watch the kids and she couldn't go out, so she's gonna be pissed if she wakes up and sees you in here with me."

Buck looks down at her thighs and hopes that she just shut up and show him to her room.

"Well stop talking so much." He then nods up the steps to insinuate for her to show him the way.

Buck and Gena enter her dark room. Her mattress is on top of her box spring without a bed frame. Buck feels sorry for her and makes a mental note to buy her a nice bedroom set to stunt on her broke as boyfriend.

Gena puts on her Lyfe Jennings play list. As Lyfe Jennings and Fantasia explore their hypotheticals,

Buck begins to explore the reality in front of him. He sits down in front of her, pulls down her yellow tights, and smells her womanhood.

He does his best to keep calm and make sure he performs. He kisses her belly button, and works his way down to her already leaking box. She throws her leg over his shoulder and he goes to work, licking her wall in circles while her fluids soak into his beard.

He lays her down and finds her clitoris with his tongue while lifting the hood of her va jay with his left hand. He sticks his index finger and middle finger of his free hand and rubs the top of her va jay using a "come here" motion.

As she has her first orgasm, she lets out a way too loud moan while clutching the back of his head. CeCe opens the door and begins to berate her.

"You loud as shit yo! You gonna wake these damn... Is that Buck? You corny as shit yo?"

She slams the door. Gena snickers, and Buck is happy she didn't shut the session down. She pushes his head back down. After making her cum one more time, he stands up and notices the grin on her face. She's confident in her twirly game, and he sees it all over her face.

She grabs his manhood with both hands, and twist while simultaneously sucking the soul out of him. Thanks to his rumps with Lisa Lips, he was able to maintain his composure, and hang on for a nice minute before her technique proved too much and let bust in her mouth. She swallowed every drop.

He pushes her onto the bed and slides into her.

"O my God".

He whispered in her ear, not believing how good she felt. He throws her healthy legs over his shoulders and stands up in it like a champ. He pounds away while looking down at the juices oozing out of her va jay.

As he releases the rest of his worries inside of her, a loud thud hits the door. He gets his pistol off the floor, and peeps out the doors, only to find a shoe that CeCe threw at the door. They both laugh.

Buck puts on his boxer briefs, and bulls a Backwood out of his pocket.

"You got a light in here?"

Gena leans over his lap, and grabs a lighter off the floor. He takes notice of how good she makes dimples look, and sparks his Backwood. He feels her stares.

"Why you staring at me?" She smiles and places her head in his lap. "Everybody says you have a wife, is it true?"

Buck knowing it's best to keep it a hundred, does just that.

"Yeah it's true. We're married under Islam."

Gena not about to capitulate responds.

"Well I guess you have two wives now." They both share a laugh.

The next morning Buck is paying his mother his usual morning visit, before going to pick up Seek. He approaches her in the kitchen cooking breakfast for herself and his little sister.

"Smelling good woman. What you cooking?"

Ma Dukes smiles always happy to see her oldest boy.

"I'm making some biscuits, bacon, and eggs for me and the rug rat. You want some?"

Buck not about to miss a meal responds.

"Well since you asked, I'll definitely take some of them eggs and biscuits, but you can miss me with that pork."

Ma Dukes not acknowledging his religion as usual, shoots back.

"Niggah I raised ya black ass on pork."

A semi irritated Buck lightens the mood.

"Yep, and I raised right up on off of it."

Ma Dukes shakes her head, and smirks, before putting him on a mission.

"Do me a favor and take your brother school shopping this morning. He knows what he wants already so let him pick out his own clothes."

Knowing where she was getting at, Buck says.

"No problem but he's killing me with these Dickies and shell tops everyday tho, but I got it. Tell him to come on. I'll be in the car."

Buck and his little brother, Malcolm enter a crowded mall. Malcolm clearly got off on one of his early morning weed smoking sessions, making Buck a little uncomfortable knowing everybody will see how high his young ass is.

"Let's hit footlocker first so we can get you some trees."

Malcolm already knowing his angle says.

"Ard, but I need some shells too tho." Buck laughs to himself knowing his stunt wouldn't have worked.

Malcolm catches Buck off guard when he says.

"I heard Flea is in the trap now. I'm trying to go out there and get my own money too. Me and Flea is the same age, and I know my way around the trap just as well as him. So, what's the difference?"

Buck, kind of pissed that his little bro felt the need to be in the streets, tries to help him see his position.

"Man, the difference is you're my little brother. My blood. You only see what you think is the good, but it gets dark out there, and if there's no need for you to be out there then you shouldn't even want to be out there.

Mommy would never forgive me if I put you on and you got killed. You're covered bro, so get that out of your head. Don't do as I do, do as I say."

Buck drops his little brother off at his moms' house, and goes to pick up Seek.

Seek comes out of his apartment with half of his face swollen.

"Fuck happened to ya face bro?"

Seek shakes his head.

"Man, after you left this lame ass niggah from 49th street, felt the need to grandstand in front of Taryn. I think he was fucking the bitch, and got jealous when he saw her wit me. Anyway, this niggah and two other lames strolled me."

Buck full of rage that they would even try that with his right-hand man, snaps.

"Why the fuck didn't you call me?"

Seek trying to keep cool, and save face.

"Bro I got it. To be honest it's kind of funny to me. These niggahs still out here fighting. I got a wakeup call for them tho."

Already putting his game plan together, Bucks responds. "Naw. WE, got something for them."

Buck turns up his stereo as Omillio Sparks screams over the hook-on Beanie Sigel's "Tales of A Hustler"...

"In this life you not promised tomorrow so take the bitter with the sweet and maintain - In these vicious streets - Carry ya heat - Keep ya mind on ya money - Life's a gamble - Everybody got a number homie - Tales of Hustler".

Buck and Seek pull up in Buck's old Buick that Seek gave him when he first got out of the juvie joint. Seek way too relaxed for Buck's liking asks.

"Damn you still got this piece of shit?"

Buck trying to stay focused, nonetheless entertains the dumb ass question.

"Yeah I tucked it away a while back. I was gonna give it to my little brother, but Ma Dukes wasn't having it. Look on the back seat."

Seek turns around and takes note of the K back there.

"I grabbed that off of Chicken Man. We're gonna run his play on this one, the same one we ran when I first landed."

They pull up to the light not noticing the unmarked car following them. They pull up to the light and notice two of the opposition out there in front of the Chinese store. Buck pulls by slowly letting them take notice of his old car. He spins the corner.

"Jump out bro, you known the routine."

Seek jumps out and gives it a minute before spinning the corner. He sees the two lames staring down the old Buick and creep up behind them. As seek raises the K, Buck notices a marked car behind him. He slams on the horn and pulls up to pick Seek up. Seek jumps in and the chase is on.

"Damn this fucking Buick is slow as shit. Throw the stick out the window when I turn this corner."

Buck turns the corner and bangs out into a double-parked car. Him and Seek are arrested. Handcuffed once again to the exact same table, in walks punk ass Detective Jenkins. Buck notices the gray hairs that wasn't there before and as usual doesn't miss his shot.

"That Just 4 Men not doing you no justice huh?"

Jenkins not fazed by the smart assed comment.

"Good, so you remember me. Then you remember that I told you we'd be talking again. It's been some years young Buck. O Yeah, my fault... Derrick, call you Derrick, right? Well Derrick here we are having that talk."

Buck getting nervous and figuring he'd better stop the bullshit and wrap this up.

"Man, listen. You doing all the talking. Why am I in homicide any way when all you got is a gun case? Let me see the judge so I can make bail."

Detective Jenkins gears up to drop the bomb he's been waiting years to drop.

"Good observation Derrick. Well as you know, we don't give two fucks about drugs and gun cases. Us long coats like to focus on good ole homicides.

Murder, like the ones in the first degree. Now that I we're on the same page let's proceed. I have a witness that puts you on the scene when your boy Rahman was killed. He also puts a gun in your hand. Your boy Reef? Yeah, he was out there.

He didn't talk then but he caught himself a domestic case against his baby's momma. And guess who he's telling on in exchange for a shorter sentence? Correcto Mundo my friend. Your black ass."

Buck not believing he's just been charged with this old ass body, is transferred to the county jail, where he runs into Seek on quarantine. They embrace, and Seek gets straight to business.

"Damn bro that shit almost got dark. I appreciate you sacrificing for me, and not leaving me for dead."

Buck anxious to pull his right hand up on everything.

"That's what we do bro. It's no way you would have beat that body had the state witnesses been the

PPD. All in all, we got bigger problems. Jenkins was following us that day waiting to pick me up on a warrant.

This niggah Reef got booked and decided to out a body on me, so I'm gonna have the line bail you out, and I'm gonna need you to clean that up for me."

Seek glad he didn't get grinded up for not having bail money.

"I got you bro. Anything"

They walk over to a table and sit down. The smell of the unit is overwhelming them. A mixture of body fluids from the fiends going through withdrawals, to county soap. Buck states the obvious.

"How the fuck we go from a night in the 5200 club to these baggy ass orange jumpsuits? I need out of here ASAP."

After a few months Seek's detainer is finally lifted and he's eligible to make bail. He and Buck are talking while awaiting in the phone line. Seek asks Buck.

"How did they charge you for that old ass body anyway, ain't it a statute of limitations on that."

Buck unwittingly responds.

"Absolutely not. Bodies never go away. They can come back fifty years from now, and charge you up."

Little did Buck know his comment would scare his best friend off. Seek would make bail and never speak to Buck again, however they would have one last show down before parting ways.

While standing in the back of the phone line, three inmates walk to the front of the line.

"You kidding me? These weirdos really just walked to the front of the line?" Buck yells out. " My man! what the fuck we don't exist back here?"

The inmate turns around with his double chin hanging, and stained T-shirt under that bright ass jumpsuit, and spews.

"Not to me niggah, you ain't special."

A furious Buck, can only imagine what he would do to his fat ass on the other side of these walls, but decides to try his best to tear his fat ass apart on this side. He exchanges that familiar look with Seek as they pull their bangas out of their socks, and go to work.

First Taste of Solitary

BUCK'S FIRST STINT IN SOLITARY CONFINEMENT...

Buck is now in the hole for the first time in his life. Word spread fast about his wreck and people are joeing him who he doesn't even know.

The guards finally approach his cell in order to take him to his visit, in which he's been waiting on. The inmates start to bang the doors as they always do and yelling.

One inmate who Buck didn't know from a can of paint bent down and screamed under the door insuring he was heard loud and clear.

"Bucky Yanno. Who came to see you, niggah? Make sure she flashes a titty in the booth."

The guard, Officer Black was a real dick head. The most miserable of miserable fuck boys you'd ever met. Slightly overweight, with a chip on his shoulder, due to the fact his brother was gunned downed like a dog. He hated all prisoners, and didn't miss an opportunity to make life as miserable as his.

"You ready or what Fam? You taking all day."

Knowing how heavy a dick head he was, Buck decides to try and play it cool.

"Yeah I'm ready".

Only to be shocked at what was next. "I can't tell. You still have your clothes on."

Not knowing where he was getting at and felling disrespected Buck shot back.

"Fuck am I supposed to go on the visit naked?"

Black narrowed his eyes and shot right back.

"You gotta strip before leaving the cell. You strip going in and you strip going out. So, bust it open for the black man."

Before Buck could respond a random inmate yelled out.

"Aye Black!!!". Officer Black taking the bait. "Fuck you want? I'm busy". The inmate fires. " You gay as shit... BITCH!!!"

Buck and the rest of the pod burst out in laughter.

"Ha ha ha. You just laughed you way out of a visit dick head."

Buck snaps.

"You a bitch bro! Ya lame ass can't live in my city, it's impossible niggah. Somebody would have been blew ya fuckin brains out. You running around here like you judge and fucking jury. Niggah FUCK YOU!!!"

MONTHS PASS BY…

Buck has had no contact from the streets. He's baffled as to where everybody is at. All the love he'd expected hasn't show up. His thoughts are interrupted by an inmate yelling on the door.

"Main man in thirty-two cell you from seventeenth street?"

Thirty-two cell responds.

"Yeah why where you from homie?"

Like clockwork.

"You know where I'm from pussy. I'm the one who robbed you and took them Guccis off ya feet."

The entire block erupts into laughter, and begin to kick the doors.

After a few more months pass, Buck is finally allowed a visit from his sweetheart Butta. She entered the 4×4 visiting booth, and Buck's heart just dropped.

She was so sweet and so beautiful. She removed her niqab so that Buck could see her face. He was a sucker for her smile and prostration mark on her forehead and she knew it. When she smiles and her dimples would become blood shot red. She really had his heart. She was the soft to his hard.

Complete opposites. He'd never even heard her curse. In fact, he would make it his mission to get her to curse just one time and it never worked. He would plead.

"Just say bitch, one time. I just want to hear how you sound cussing." And she would shoot him down every time.

He knew he had to do better by her when given another chance. She sat down and asked him.

"Why have you been refusing my visits?"

He assures her that wasn't the case and explain what he was up against.

"Really? You know that I would never refuse your visit. This gay ass guard has been shooting my visits down. He wants me to get butt ass naked every time I leave the cell and go in it. He fuckin gay."

Not wanting to argue she ignores his potty mouth.

"Okay well I'm happy to see you; did you miss me?"

Buck knowing how much he loves making her smile says. "Absolutely. You know what I miss most right?"

Butta flashes her signature blush, and says.

"What nasty?" Buck ready's himself to make mental note of her laugh to come.

"That fried fish and home fries your grand mom used to make on Sundays."

Butta slaps his arm and they both laugh.

Her serious face returns really quick, and it's coupled with blatant worry.

"Buck everybody is worried that you may never come home again."

The truth in her words hit Buck like a ton of bricks, and his reality is on his lap.

"I'm gonna be honest with you. Nothing is guaranteed, and you know that. I don't even want to think about dying behind these walls.

I mean I'm literally sleeping with mice, and roaches. This shit is a nightmare. All I can say is I'm doing my best to secure my chances, and if things go our way, I'm gonna try my best to be done with the streets.

I know it comes off as jail talk, but I promise I'm gonna try. The shit isn't normal."

Butta wanting to trust her husband's words responds.

"You can work like everybody else. It seems like you can't see beyond what you already know. Well you know that a couple of your friends are driving tow trucks now, and you know that works, so why not try that?"

Buck knowing she's right agrees.

"I promise you I'm gonna do my best. It just seems like shit always just comes my way, even in here. I just refuse to be anybody's victim. I rather be Judged By 12 than carried by 6 any day."

Butta not one to not voice her opinion, stands her ground.

"But why does it always have to be you? It seems like you're always the one who goes too far and takes the hardest fall."

Buck trying to be the last word in.

"That's not true. You remember S., you remember Rahman, and there's many more in worst positions than me. I just refuse to be Rahman. He died with his gun in his lap. He knew it was on and he was slipping. I refuse for that to be me."

Buck was interrupted by the guard.

"Visiting hour up Davis."

Buck drops his head and watches the guards eyeing his wife as she leaves the visiting room. Flaming he's escorted back to the hole.

Back in population Buck is watching TV in the day room with one of his youngins from the block named Mista. Mista was a young hammer, but had no ambition. All he wanted to do was get high and play with pistols.

Mista interrupts Buck watching the Maury Povich show.

"Buck. Tell me that ain't O. from 49th street."

Buck takes a good look and affirms Mista's observation. He sends Mista to strap up, and tells him to meet back in his cell. Mista enter Buck's cell with his banga in tow.

"He's going into the multipurpose room with the Poppies. The Poppies twist with us so they won't back his play against us, so we're gonna... Hold up. This dick head is getting in the shower. He didn't even map the block out before jumping in the water. We gonna take him deep then. You ready, Mista?"

Giggling nervously, Mista nods, and they enter the shower and stab former nemesis, O. The guards rush the pod and mace everybody.

Adaptability

BUCK'S SECOND STINT IN THE HOLE...

"C. O!!! THIS MACE IS BURNING MY FUCKIN EYES!!!"

Buck yells under the doors not realizing how he's beginning to adapt to his environment. The guard assures him that medical will be around soon, and to be patient. Another inmate decides to get involved in the drama by yelling.

"Black you a fuckin lie. I see you smiling as if the shit is funny. Aye Buck. Just ride it out soldier. Don't use soap either, it just makes it worse."

Months pass by and Buck is becoming more and more used to dealing with his environment. The mice and roaches don't bother him as much.

The 24/7 kicking screaming and banging actually help him sleep better now, and the inconsistent contact with the streets are becoming normal to him. He sits by the door waiting for his next dose of amusement.

Right in time an inmate named Tori, who does nothing but write raps about jail gets on the door.

"Hold up! I wrote some new shit! Hold up!"

The block quiets down in order for everybody to hear Tori's rap for the night.

"Y'all ready? This shit called, 'Stab Em'. I said, I'll stab em in a minute, stab em in an hour, stab em like Buck stabbed O., in the shower..." The block erupts.

Buck shares in the laugh with his celly, Hell Rell. Hell Rell was a real live wire. He reminded Buck of Dez on every level. They even had the same look. The only difference was that dumb ass box style hair cut that Hell Rell was rocking.

It was a weird relationship, because Buck knew he wouldn't spend more the than five minutes in Hell Rell's company on the other side of these walls, but somehow was just fine with him locked down 24/7.

He was beginning to learn more and more of changes within himself that he was accepting in order to not focus on the reality in front of him.

Hell Rell notices him zoning out.

"You good bro?"

Buck reluctantly answers, knowing this dude wouldn't understand where his mind was at.

"You know what's crazy bro? Shit in here is the same out there. It's like I'm damned if I do and damned if I don't. Had I seen the niggah and not moved first, then it would have been my name in Tori's rap tonight as the one getting banged out.

I chose to push first, and now it's just more drama that never ends. I'm getting tired of this shit bro. When do I get a break?

A fuckin day off. Just one. This pressure is every day, 24 fuckin 7 no breaks. It's like once we start this shit, we're stuck. I followed the only route I knew, and it's just a chain reaction."

Hell Rell hoping he shuts up so he can ask for his batteries in order to light his cigarette cuts in.

"You getting a conscious on me, bro? At the end of the day this is the life we chose. We have to accept this shit, and play to win.

Fuck that niggah. If his feelings are hurt then just stab his ass again when y'all cross paths and this time make sure you enjoy that shit.

We're cut from a different cloth. It is what it is. Let me get a light."

Buck shakes his head, and gives him the batteries.

"Enjoy ya'self."

Ma Dukes is awakened by the sound of her front door being kicked in.

"Police!!! We got a warrant for Malcolm Ford."

A startled Ma Dukes hugs her baby girl.

"He's not here. A warrant for what?"

The officer drops the last words she wanted to hear.

"First degree murder. It seems like you breed murderers around here. We're gonna be kicking this door in on a regular basis, so it's best he turns himself in sooner than later."

Days pass by and Ma Dukes decides to pay Buck a visit along with his little sister. He lights up when she runs up and gives him a hug and kiss. Ma Dukes puts her on the spot.

"Yeah, hug your brother. As much as you ask about him, I'm glad, now you finally get to see him."

They sit down, and Buck lowers his head.

"I heard about Malcolm. I know he's following my footsteps, and I'm sorry we're putting you through this. I really don't know what else to say."

Ma Dukes lifts his head.

"There's nothing to say regarding what's already happened. Both if my sons are locked away for murder. For taking someone else's sons away from their mother.

What y'all failed to realize is that y'all actions would affect more than just y'all. I'm scared to even leave my house, not knowing if someone is out there waiting for me, in order to get back at you.

I tried to keep you straight, and you just refused to listen. Now you both are facing forever behind these walls. How do you think I feel?

How do you think it feels to have not one but two sons who're labelled murderers? The shit hurts, and y'all are sending me to an early grave."

Buck not knowing what to say, just drops his head once again. Ma Dukes picks it back up.

"You have to figure it out. This has to stop. Every time I speak to your wife, she tells me you're in the hole. You're still harming others. When will it stop?

Know that I love you, but the day has to come where you grow up, and start living for other than yourself."

Buck holding back tears. "I love you too..."

Ma Dukes needed answers that he just couldn't provide.

"What did I do wrong? Did I not try my best to provide? Did you not have a roof over your head? Food in your mouth?"

Buck thought back to the nights where his stomach would beg to differ, but knew not to throw fuel on the fire.

"Did you not have clothes on your back? What happened?"

Realizing that she made her point, Ma Dukes chose to let up.

"I know your trial is coming up, and we will be there to support you. Once again, I love you, we love you, and I need you to get it together. Do it for us. It's our turn to have your unconditional love. You've given it to the streets for far too long. It's our turn now."

Buck agrees and hugs her and his little sister tight, and watches them walk out of the visiting room.

Trial

TRIAL…

 Buck enters the courtroom and takes a quick look behind him to acknowledge his friends and family who came to support him. He makes a mental note that everybody there is his family, and his wife's family along with a few neighbors who'd watch him grow up.

He thinks to himself

Man not a niggah from the block, not even Seek. I fed these dudes for years and not one showed face. Rahman warned me about these dudes, but it's good. Now I know.

The Judge enters the courtroom, and the Court Clerk addresses the courtroom.

"Please be seated. Your Honor, this is the matter of Derrick Davis versus the Commonwealth."

The judge takes the bench. Buck's surprised at the number of black faces in the courtroom. The judge being a middle-aged black man who'd seemed incapable of showing any emotion. The assistant district attorney was also a middle-aged black woman, who wore the tightest red mini skirt and a pair of six inch come fuck me heels.

She must have been done wrong by a black man because she smiles at everybody in the courtroom until she reached Buck.

The disgust was evident. Even the entire jury was black. The only white face in the courtroom was Buck's lawyer. An overweight Jewish man.

The assistant district attorney stands and begins her opening arguments.

"May it please the court? Ladies and gentlemen of the jury. Good afternoon. His Honor has given me the opportunity today to present to you an opening statement.

You're going to be hearing direct testimony, testimony providing beyond a reasonable doubt that the defendant, willfully gunned down the victim in cold blood. The Commonwealth has the burden of proof in this case, and the Commonwealth intends to meet that burden, beyond a reasonable doubt."

While the ADA is putting on her show Buck inquires his lawyer about securing him a plea deal. He had three years to do so, but swore up and down that he would beat this case, and get Buck back on the streets.

The judge then instructs the defense that it's their turn for opening statements. Buck's lawyer stands up to address the jury looking a hot mess. His suit is wrinkled, and the judge has to force him to tuck his shirt in, due to a portion hanging out the front. Buck can only wonder where his twenty-five grand went that he gave this clown.

He addresses the jury.

"Good morning your Honor, ladies and gentlemen of the jury.

Yes, the Commonwealth does have the burden of proof beyond a reasonable doubt in this case. Question. How do you prove murder with no weapon? How do you send someone to jail for the rest of their life, based on the testimony of a sole witness, a witness who didn't come forth until four years later, and not until after he'd found himself facing serious jail time for assaulting a woman?

A woman who bore his child? The answer is you don't. You simply can't. My client is not guilty, and we pray your verdict represents that."

After a long emotional week, and the trial is finally coming to an end. All they have to do is make closing arguments, and wait on the jury's verdict.

An anxious Buck sits back and prepares to listen to closing arguments. The ADA stands and straightens out her tight ass everyday skirt.

"Ladies and gentlemen of the jury. We have presented overwhelming evidence and proved beyond a reasonable doubt the guilt of Mr. Davis. The law isn't as the defense would like you to think. A reasonable doubt, is not perfect, it's exactly what we said it was, and that's reasonable.

As I look at the faces on this jury, and within this courtroom, I see faces who know all too well, what's sitting in front of us. We live with it on a daily basis. This is your chance to do your part and uphold the law.

Do your duty to your community and remove the likes of Mr. Davis from your neighborhoods. We ask that you convict him of first-degree murder, and nothing less."

Buck now notices why his lawyer told him not to pick an all-black jury. The reverse racism is real, and it just bit him in the ass. His lawyer stands and begins to address the jury.

"Ladies and gentlemen of the jury it has been a long week, and you have heard some very emotional, and very graphic testimony.

I'm asking that you base your verdict off of the law, and contrary to what the ADA said the law is perfect. How can we, members of society, upholders of the Constitution; literally hang someone's life on laws that are not perfect? You get it wrong and this young man goes to jail and stays there until he dies.

Who wants that on their plate? This is a long cry from a home run, there's so many flaws in the case, and I ask that you find him, this young man, this human being, regardless of what you may think of him, not guilty on all charges. Thanks."

Buck pleased with his representation but still pissed he didn't secure him a plea bargain, sits patiently waiting on the verdict. The jury foreman stands and a informs the court they've reached a verdict. The judge asked him how does he find, and the skinny foreman, who could benefit from some Proactive, states.

"We the jury, in the case of Derrick Davis, versus the Commonwealth, finds him guilty of murder in the first degree."

The courtroom erupts, Buck gets dizzy. He can't muster the courage to turn around and face his loved one's tears. The judge dismisses the jury, and imposes a sentence of life without the possibility of parole on Buck.

Now twenty-three years old Buck is being transferred to the state penitentiary. He's deep in thought trying to figure out what's next for him.

The old prison bus, nicknamed the Bluebird, sounds as if it's gonna break down at any minute, and the constant complaints from the other prisoners being transported, are driving him crazy.

Really? This is the last I'm gonna see my city? Through a gated window, shackled from waste to feet, on this piece if shit as bus? Really? These dudes playing around and crying over these light ass sentences, and I'm entering these mountains waiting to fuckin die, I'm ready to burst. It seems like I'm the only one wit all this fuckin time.

Butta cried so hard when they found me guilty. My chest hurts just thinking about her wails. Then this ugly ass fuckin clerk had the nerve to kick her out the courtroom. They didn't kick that niggah's folks out and they were crying throughout the entire trial. How the fuck was that fair?

But I'm the evil one, I'm the monster, I'm the murderer. Fuck out of here. These people just killed me. Death by means of incarceration. They rocking shit on a daily basis.

My body count ain't shit compared to the court's. I make one bad decision and they have the right and rank to play god, and kill me? I can't believe this shit. How do I do a life sentence? I'm just gonna appeal this thing This is my last shot and I have to make it count.

Life w/ Life

TWO YEARS PASS...

Buck enters the yard and hits the weight pit. It has to be every bit of 100 degrees out, but he needs that rec to curb his stress. Bank Head spots him and heads his way.

Bank Head was one of the younger dudes from his block, a quiet li'l dude, who knew how to stack his cheese.

Buck actually used to like the li'l niggah, until he showed his true colors. His big brother, Cheeks was a hammer and ended up catching a life sentence also.

Buck had heard that Bank Head wasn't doing shit to help his own brother, but would run to him every time niggahs was on his ass out there. So, any love Buck had for the lame was nonexistent.

Bank Head approached blurts the first thing that comes to his mind.

"Damn bro we miss you out there. Shit hasn't been the same. How is ya appeal coming along?"

Buck shakes his head and replies.

"I can't tell. It's been over six years, and I haven't heard a word from y'all dudes.

Shit Ma Dukes tell me y'all don't even check in on her. I heard about Cheeks tho. I heard he's not feeling you either.

All in all, I'm still waiting on my opinion from the courts. It's been a few years, but the wheels of justice tend to move at a snail's pace."

Bank Head not being one for confrontation accepts the critique.

"My fault bro, I didn't know what this shit was hitting for until I came through here but I'm gonna play my part when I slide homie. I promise. Oh yah, guess what? Ma Dukes quit drinking."

He knew that would make Buck smile. His mom would give Buck the biggest hugs whenever she saw him, and Buck would soak them up every time. Buck had more pseudo mothers than he could count. Buck decides to slide.

"I'm gone for now bro, I gotta call wifey up."

A surprised Bank asks. "Butta? She still around?"

Buck refusing to miss his chance to take another shot quip.

"Of course. You know these chicks are more loyal than these niggahs. Me and her connected for life. Loyalty my man."

After a quick shower, Buck is waiting on mail call. His celly, Beezy also a lifer is doing the same.

Beezy was a tall bald head skinny dude, with the nastiest scar down the right side of his face. His shady ways had caught up to him, and some bloods splashed him, and left him with that scar.

The guard approaches the cell, and give Buck his legal mail. He'd been preparing for better or worse, so he felt ready. After reading it, he walks out the cell and gets on the phone to call Butta. She answers as always.

"Asalaamu Alaikum." Buck responds dryly. " Wa Alaikum Salaam. So, I got my opinion just now and they denied my appeal."

Butta breaks down into tears.

"I thought they were gonna grant it? What happened? Listen I know you and I know what you're gonna say. I'm not going anywhere."

Buck cuts her off.

"Butta life means life for me. You've given me some of your best years. Like you said, you know me. What does that say about me, if I just hold onto you, and prevent you from living your life.

You don't have kids, and you don't have forever to start a family. Listen you know how much I love you; you've stood by me when those I've held closest have abandoned me, but we have to let go. I love You."

Buck hangs up and would never speak with Butta again.

He returns to the cell, and is confronted by his cellmate.

"So, what happened? You get some news you could use or what?"

Buck not really trying to talk, and trying to wrap his head around what this means, responds.

"Naw, they denied me. I just hung up wit wifey, and had to walk away from that." His cellmate being the idiot he is, unsympathetically quips. "Bro I told you, these bitches ain't shit..."

Buck snaps and breaks for the first time. He puts hands and feet all over his celly. The guards rush in, and restrain him.

He's taken to the hole. He's placed in a cage with only his boxers on. He's then approached by a 6'5 300 pounds of lard guard. The bulge of snuff poking out the side of his jaw, screams redneck and Buck realizes this is the beginning of a new world for him. Buck asks the guard.

"What time do y'all do calls?"

The guard looks up from the jump suit he was holding surprised he's being questioned.

"Listen you don't get no damn phone calls, nor no fuckin visits. If you know what's best for your ashy ass, you'd shut the fuck up and wait on your orders, now take your boxers off."

Two more guards approach the cage one holding a video camera. Buck feels a sense of security being as tho it was being recorded, and he removes his boxers. The guard steps closer.

"Lift your hands, run your fingers through your beard, lift your dick, lift your dick, lift your dick."

Buck feels the rage building and tries his utmost to tame his demons. "I did lift my dick".

The guard spits a wad of snuff into his paper cup, and shoots back.

"That's your nuts and your dick, retard. Just lift your dick. Turn around, left foot, right foot, bend over, spend em, again, again. I want to see out ya mouth through your ass."

Buck snaps.

"Man, fuck THAT, and fuck you. Do what y'all gotta do."

Buck puts his boxers back on knowing what's next.

The guards smile. One leaves a shortly returns with a riot shield. They open the cage and all three rush Buck.

Bending his fingers, slamming his head into the concrete, and stripping him completely naked. They cuff him, and continue to dehumanize him.

"You, smart ass nigger. You're going in number nine cell with the Bus Driver."

The Bus Driver was a known child molester, and homosexual. He got his name from picking up kids at bus stops, and raping them. He wasn't you're run of the mill, frail, and timid child molester.

He was 5'10 and cut like a bag of dope. Buck knew he would have to put hands on him immediately, and this would give the guards reason to "restrain" him once again but he had no choice.

"Crack nine cell!"

Bus Driver is standing at the back of the cell smiling when the guard carried Buck to the cell. Buck's still naked and has never felt more humiliated. They remove his cuffs and the fight is on.

Buck jumps up, and goes straight for him. He throws an overhand right, but Bus Driver goes straight in for a Pittsburgh Jack, and grabs his legs.

Buck is pissed that he has to wrestle with this freak while naked, but within minutes the three overweight pigs are back on top of him restraining him once again.

They shackle him once more and escorted him to the "side pocket". The side pocket was a hole inside the hole.

Buck had heard tales of it but never believed it existed. It was one tier, three cells, one shower and no cameras. If they wanted to kill you, that would be the perfect spot.

While walking past of the cells Buck saw an old man on the door. He thought he was tripping, because this dude looked like a mentally ill version of Frederick Douglas. He was smiling ear to ear, just standing on the door.

They tossed Buck into a single cell next to the Frederick Douglas look alike. The cell was completely empty. No mattress, no linen, no clothes, nothing. The air had to be on every bit 40° if not lower.

After the guards left, the old man yelled over.

"Just hold on youngy, it's gonna get harder before it gets easier. I've been up here for five years. You gonna have to learn real quick when you can win and, when you don't stand a rat's ass.

One, look around and should see that you don't stand a rats ass."

Rock Bottom????

Months pass, and slowly Buck earns clothes and showers once in a blue moon. However, the guards constantly forge write-ups on him in order to bury him in the hole.

"Davis! You have mail, it's a write-up, for threatening an officer. Buck heatedly defends himself, but gets nowhere.

"Tell it to the hearing examiner".

A year later and the write-ups have slowed up, and Buck is holding on by a thread. Ole School, yells over.

"Youngy I got these books that I want you to take a look at. I'm gonna send them over. Tell me what you think after you're done with them."

Ole School sent Buck some books on black history. After a few weeks, Ole School checks in.

"Youngy! Did you ever read them books? If so let me know where ya head is at."

Buck still soaking up everything he'd read, hesitantly responds.

"I never learned about slavery, Jim Crow and Civil Rights. I mean I heard about it vaguely, but not in a way that I understood.

Learning about these things now has me kind of fucked up. I'm feeling... ambivalent."

Ole School, laughs.

"Ambivalent? I see you're getting your vocabulary up."

Not wanting to lose his train of thought.

"Naw seriously Ole School. I feel like I let these people down, like I disgraced them. It's funny because the same thing I was raised in the streets not to do, is exactly what I did.

My old head is doing twenty years, my best friend was gunned down, and they both sacrificed for our block, yet nobody appreciated the work we put in. I feel like this is the same thing, but oppose to us sacrificing in a way that sets our people back, they sacrificed for some good, to help advance our people, and I'm the fake one who didn't honor their sacrifices.

These men and women died for me, and my generation, and I shitted on their work. Even kids died in the name of freedom, and I just gave mine away. I feel like some shit Ole School.

Now look at me, I don't even have an option to turn it around. I'm property now. State property. We might as well be slaves the way they got us."

Ole School takes the opportunity to share more of his wisdom with Buck.

"Funny you should say that. Read this."

He slides a folder under the door to Buck.

Buck reading aloud...

"Neither Slavery nor Involuntary Servitude, Shall Be Lawful Within the United States, Except, As A Punishment for A Crime... What the fuck is this, Ole School?"

Ole School Pulls his chair close to the door. Folds his hands into a ball, and rests his chin on them.

"That there is the 13th Amendment of the United States Constitution. That there Youngy is the law of this land. So, you were right we are slaves, and it's all 100% legal.

This country was built of the backs of our people, and they still profit off of slavery even today. Look at us. They give us just enough food to keep is alive, just enough heat to keep us alive, two showers a week, and the same one set of clothes for years on end.

Without us where would these hillbillies be? When the coal mines were shut down, and all the plants closed these people were out on their ass. So, they built prisons in every stick mountain in the state.

Without us prisons don't exist, and their bills don't get paid. Did you notice that damn near everybody in here is black?

So, they designed laws, and environments that put us here and keep us here. They design school systems, which deprive us, and secure their own. They separate us, dump us in the ghettos, and projects, put delis on every corner, fly crack into our neighborhoods. How do you think it gets there? I don't know not one person with a private plane. Hell, I don't know one person who has ever left the country.

They keep us ignorant, Youngy, but now you know, and now you don't have an excuse. Find a way to give back, and do it.

Find a way to spare the next li'l dude walking in your footsteps, and spare him, spare him before he's in somebody's prison, and the next product of his environment. This is me, doing what I can with what I got. It's your turn."

Sixteen months pass, and Buck is still in the side pocket. He's trying to work his way out, and once again is in deep thought.

Man these fuckers won't give me no toilet paper, soap, or shower. What the fuck is this? I need out this hole, and now. I'm fuckin talking to myself now. Ole School hears me when I'm in full fledged conversation with myself, and I know that he doesn't say anything in order to spare my feelings.

I'm hungry as shit too. All I need is some hope. I just need something or someone to hold onto and give me some hope. Nobody is writing me, no pictures...

nothing. This has to be the worst way to die. Dudes on death row even have TVs, phone calls, and commissary. I can't even g a book unless Ole Schools sends it to me. Please give me a break.

Rock Bottom!!!

TWO MONTHS LATER...

Man maybe I can get a time cut. That's too much like right tho. Fuck it, I just have to dig deep, and finish this hole time, and move from there.

The guards have been falling back lately, and not forging any write-ups on me, so I just have to man up and push through this. Aw man this dick head is working today? I know I'm burnt for my meal, so I'm not even gonna say nothing when he starts his shit. Little does he know I tucked my bread from lunch so I'll be straight tonight.

The guard enters the tier with the dinner trays.

"Trays up! On your doors, lights on now! Davis take that off your light."

Buck looks at his light and responds.

"There's nothing on my light."

The guard yells to the bubble.

"Davis refused his meals."

Buck remains silent, and doesn't feed into the trap. The seasoned guard figures him out immediately.

"You think you're smart don't you… you dumb ass nigger? You think you figured it out?"

The guard reaches into his back pocket and pulls out a prewritten write-up and slides it under the door. He laughs and walks off.

The minute he's off the range, Buck falls to his knees and cries for hours on end. Everything he'd ever done flashing before his eyes. S., Rahman, Ma Dukes, His sisters and brother, Butta, Seek, Dez, Nell, Chicken Man, Gena, CeCe, Lisa Lips, Herb, Aunty, O., Tori, Hell Rell... Everything and everybody just washing over him.

These fuckers have broken me. They fuckin got me. I lost everything, and everybody. I don't even exist anymore. The nice car, beautiful wife, long money, healthy family, are all gone. Out of sight out if mind. I'm in here getting treated and I don't have a shoulder to lean on outside of Ole School.

I own my wrongs. I lived a fucked-up life, I didn't value my own life, so how could I value other's. I've taken life and I have to take what comes with that. But am I not entitled to redemption?

This country was built on kidnapping, rape, murder, and slavery. Yet those who participated were given a shot at redemption. The world forgave this country for their sins, so why can't I get a second chance? How is this shit fair?

I've spent my lifetime focused on survival, and I lost my life to an enemy I didn't even know existed... The fuckin system. This system is far from broken, it's designed to do exactly what it's doing... I once told Butta, that I'd rather be Judged By 12, than carried by 6. Little did I know, that was a lie...

Buck hangs himself.

Ole School decides to yell over.

"Youngy! I just read my newspaper from yesterday. The United States Supreme Court has passed a law, stating that anybody who is sentenced to life without the possibility of parole for a crime they committed before the age of eighteen, has an unconstitutional sentence.

They're referring to y'all as juvenile lifers, and saying y'all all are getting new sentences. You're going home, Youngy!" Youngy you good? Aye C.O!!!!"

Epilogue

Mr. Davis would survive his suicide attempt, and go on to earn certifications in Child Psychology, and Health Awareness from NYU, and become the founder of his mentoring program YouthMindsMatter (www.youthmindsmatter.org). He works as a tutor, and serves as the Educational Chairman for the LIFE association at the prison he's currently incarcerated in.

On May 3rd, 2019 Mr. Davis received a second sentencing hearing and after some emotional testimony the Judge agreed to give Mr. Davis a second chance and resentenced him to a term of 21years to Life. Mr. Davis is now eligible for parole in the year 2027. To listen to the live-in court testimony from Mr. Davis at his hearing please join his blog @ www.s-stop.com and click the YouTube link.

About the Author

Derrick Davis is the founder of YouthMindsMatter (see YouthMindsMatter.org); a mentoring program dedicated to uplifting at risk youth within impoverished communities by means of education.

His experiences growing up in impoverished neighborhoods, and spending his entire adulthood incarcerated, motivated him to write "Judged By 12", in hopes of giving readers a glimpse of everyday hardships that underrepresented youth endure daily. He also blogs @ www.S-STOPP.com in order to further assist those engaged in the struggle against systematic oppression.

Mr. Davis has been incarcerated since October 1st, 2006 at a state correctional facility in Pennsylvania. He was originally sentenced to Life without the possibility of parole, and on May 3rd, 2019 after a successful appeal, Mr. Davis had his sentence reduced to a term of 21 years. He's now eligible for parole in the year 2027.

He truly believes that change is possible through hard work and dedication. He spends his days indulged in work with YouthMindsMatter, writing for his blog, and preparing for his return to society. Feel free to contact him through one of these available avenues:

Contact Mr. Davis at:

SCI Dallas
Derrick Davis #KF3839
PO Box 33028
ST Petersburg, FL 33733

Or Email him by setting up an account
@www.connectnetwork.com
For "Select A State", Choose " Pennsylvania "
For "Select a Facility" Choose "Pennsylvania
Department of Corrections" or "PA/DOC"
In the "Search Criteria" Box enter "KF3839".

Made in the USA
Coppell, TX
13 February 2021